the duck and the mēan pig

a mother duck and her nīne little ducks went fōr a walk. a big mēan pig met them on the rōad. shē tōld the mother duck, "I am a mēan pig. I ēat cans and I ēat bēans. I ēat cars and I ēat tōys. I ēat beds and I ēat bugs."

the mother duck said, "I am not a can ōr a bēan ōr a car ōr a tōy. I am a duck. and I bīte pigs that ar$_e$ m$\bar{e}$$_a$n." →

    s$\bar{o}$ the pig ran. then the mother duck and her →

n$\bar{i}$n$_e$ little ducks went to the pond. →

        the end →

gōinɡ to the tōy shop

a bōy and his mother went to a tōy shop. they went to get tōys. the bōy said, "I līke tōys. I līke big tōys."

his mother said, "I do not līke big tōys. sō wē will get little tōys."

the man in the tōy shop said, "wē have a lot of tōys. wē have tōys fōr bōys. wē have tōys fōr girls.

and wē havₑ tōys fōr dogs."

the bōy said, "I am not a dog. I am a bōy. and I līkₑ big tōys."

stop

going to the tōy shop

a bōy and his mother went shopping fōr tōys.

the bōy līked big tōys. but his mother līked little tōys.

the man in the tōy shop said, "I have tōys that you will līke. they are big and little."

the bōy said, "tōys can not bē big and little."

the man said, "thēse tōys are big and little."

hē got a little tōy duck and hē māde it big.

this is the end.

the fat fox and his brother

a fat fox and his brother went into a big box.

the fat fox said, "I hāt_e to sit in a box."

his brother said, "sitting in a box is not a lot of

fun. let's hit the box. I love to hit a box."

the fat fox said, "I will hit the box with this

hand and this nōs_e and this tāil." sō hē hit and hit.

then the fat fox said, "it is getting hot in this

box. let's stop hitting." →

his brother said, "let's gō to slēēp. slēēping in a →

box is fun." sō they went to slēēp. →

this is the end. →

the other sīde of the lāke

a bug sat on the shōre of a big lāke. the bug

said, "I nēēd to get to the other sīde of this big

lāke."

but the bug did not līke to get wet. hē said, "I

līke to slēēp and I līke to rīde in a car. but I do

not līke to get wet."

the bug did not have a car and hē did not have

a beḋ. sō hē sat and sat on the shōrₑ of the lākₑ.

stop

13

the other sīde of the lāke

a bug sat and sat on the shōre of a lāke. hē did not have a car to tāke him to the other sīde.

then a big ēagle cāme and sat down on the shōre. the ēagle said, "you are sitting on the shōre and you are sad."

the bug said, "yes. I am sad. I nēēd to get to the other sīde of the lāke. I will give you a dīme."

the ēagle said, "yes. give mē a dīme and I will

tāke you to the other sīde." sō the bug gāve the

ēagle a dīme and got on the ēagle. they went ōver

the lāke.

the end

the pig that bit his leg

a little bug and a pig met on the rōₐd. the pig
said, "I can walk better than you."

the little bug said, "but I can ēat better than
you." then shē bit a log.

the pig said, "I can ēat logs better than you."
the pig went bītₑ, bītₑ, bītₑ and ātₑ the log.

the bug said, "I can bītₑ a pig better than you."

17

shē bit the pig on the leg.

the pig said, "I can do better than that." the pig

gāve his leg a big bīte.

the bug said, "you bīte pigs better than mē."

the end

the cat that talked

a girl had a little cat. shē loved her cat. shē went to the shop with her cat. shē went to the park with her cat. shē loved her cat.

the other dāy, shē was sitting with her cat in the park. shē said, "I love you, little cat. you are never bad. you are fun. but you can not talk to mē and that mākes mē sad."

the cat said, "I can talk to you."

stop

the cat that talked

a girl had a cat. shē loved her cat. shē talked to her cat.

then the cat talked to her. the girl said, "I must bē slēēping. cats can not talk."

the cat said, "you talk to mē. sō I can talk to you."

the girl gāve the cat a big hug. "I never had a

cat that talked."

the cat said, "I never had a cat that talked either." the girl and the cat talked and talked.

then ann cāme to the park. shē went up to the girl and said, "can I have that cat?"

the cat said, "I will not gō with you."

ann said, "I must bē sleēpiñg. cats do not talk. I will lēave this park." and shē did.

the end

finding some fun on the moon

some girls went to the moon in a moon ship.

a girl said, "I will find some fun." she walked

and walked. soon she came to a cow.

the moon cow said, "we have lots of fun. come

with me." the girl went with the moon cow to a

pool. the moon cow said, "this is how we have fun

on the moon." she jumped into the pool. and the

girl jumped into the pool.

the girl said, "it is fun to swim on the moon." sō
the girl and the cow went swimming every dāy. the
girl did not tell the other girls that shē went
swimming with a moon cow.

the end

will the ōld car start?

a man had an ōld car. the ōld car did not start.

sō the man went down the rōad. soon hē cāme to a rat.

the man said, "can you start an ōld car?"

the rat said, "nō. rats do not have cars."

sō the man went down the rōad. soon hē cāme to a big man. hē said, "can you start an ōld car?"

the big man said, "yes. I can but I will not. I am sitting. I never start cars if I am sitting."

the man said, "you can sit in the car if you can start it."

sō the big man got in the car and māde the car start. hē said, "I līke this ōld car. sō I will kēēp sitting in it." and hē did.

the end

the ōld man fīnds a hōrse

an ōld hōrse was in a barn. hē said, "I am sad.

I can not fīnd a man that will rīde on mē." hē

said to the cat, "have you sēēn a man that will rīde

on mē?"

the cat said, "nō."

an ōld man was walkiñg nēar the barn. hē said to

the cat, "I can not fīnd a hōrse to rīde. have you

sēēn a hōrse that I can rīde?"

the cat said, "yes. hē is in the barn."

then the ōld man walked into the barn. hē went

up to the ōld hōrse. the ōld man said, "ōld hōrse, do

you līke to gō fōr a rīde?"

the ōld hōrse said, "yes." sō the ōld man and the

ōld hōrse went rīding.

the end

rēₐd the Ītem ➔

1. if the tēₐcher says "gō," stand up. ➔

bill went fishiñg ➔

bill lĪked to gō fishiñg but hē did not get fish. the ➔

other bōys went fishiñg and got lots of fish. a big ➔

bōy got fĪve fish. a little bōy got nĪne fish. but ➔

bill did not get fish. ➔

bill was mad. hē said, "I wish I had fish lĪke the ➔

other bōys." but nō fish cāme to his līne.

    then hē had a tug on his līne. "I have a fish," hē

said. but it was not a fish. it was an ōld box.

stop

rēₐd the ītem →

1. if the tēₐcher says "now," hōld up your hand. →

bill went fishiñg →

bill went fishiñg with the other bōys. but hē did →
not get fīvₑ fish. hē did not get nīnₑ fish. hē got →
an ōld box. →

the other bōys mādₑ fun of bill. "wē havₑ fish →
and you do not. you havₑ an ōld box." →

bill was sad. hē hit the box. the top fell down. and ➤

bill said, "that box is filled with gōld." ➤

bill was not sad. hē said to the other bōys, "you ➤

have lots of fish, but I have lots of gōld." ➤

this is the end. ➤

rēₐd the Ītem ➤

1. if the tēₐcher says "now," hōld up your hands. ➤

an ōld hōrsₑ and an ēₐgle ➤

an ōld hōrsₑ and an ēₐgle sat on a hill. the ēₐgle ➤

said, "it is fun to flȳ. mȳ mother līkₑs to flȳ. mȳ ➤

brother līkₑs to flȳ. and I līkₑ to flȳ." ➤

the ōld hōrsₑ said, "can you tēₐch mē how to ➤

flȳ?" ➤

the ēₐglₑ said, "I will flȳ to the top of the

barn." and hē did.

the ōld hōrsₑ said, "I will flȳ to the top of the

barn." sō hē ran down the hill. and hē ran into the

sīdₑ of the barn. hē said, "you did not tēₐch mē

how to flȳ."

stop

read the item

1. when the teacher says "do it," pick up your book.

an old horse and an eagle

an eagle was teaching an old horse how to fly.

but the old horse did not fly. the old horse ran into

the side of a barn.

the eagle said, "I will fly to the top of the car."

and he did.

but the ōld hōrse did not flȳ to the top of the car. hē ran into the sīde of the car. hē said, "mȳ mother and mȳ brother can not flȳ. I can not flȳ."

the ēagle said, "if you can not flȳ, you can not have fun."

the hōrse said, "I can run with an ēagle on mȳ back, and that is fun."

sō the ēagle sat on the back of the ōld hōrse and the ōld hōrse ran. "yes, this is fun," they said.

the end

rēₐd the Ītems →

1. when the tēₐcher says "gō," pat your ēₐrs. →

2. when the tēₐcher says "do it," touch your fēēt. →

the red tooth brush →

a girl had a red tooth brush. shē līked her red →

tooth brush. shē brushed her tēēth six tīmes a dāy. →

shē said, "mȳ tēēth arₑ whīte. they arₑ sō whīte →

they shīne līke the moon." →

the girl had a dog, but his tēēth did not shīne.

the girl went to brush her tēēth. but shē did not sēē her tooth brush. "I do not sēē mȳ red tooth brush," shē said.

shē went to her mother. "I nēēd mȳ red tooth brush."

but her mother said, "I do not have your red tooth brush."

stop

rēₐd the Ītems →

1. when the tēₐcher says "stand up," pick up your →

book. →

2. if the tēₐcher says "now," hōld up your hands. →

the red tooth brush →

a girl lĪkₑd to brush her tēēth. shē lookₑd fōr →

her red tooth brush. but her mother did not havₑ it. →

the girl went back to her room. on the wāy, shē →

slipped and fell. shē slipped on her dog. her dog

was brushing his tēēth with her red tooth brush.

the girl said, "you have mȳ red tooth brush."

    the dog said, "I līke tēēth that shīne līke the

moon."

    the girl smīled and the dog smīled. they said,

"now wē bōth have tēēth that shīne līke the moon."

        the end

rēad the Ītems →

1. if the tēacher stands up, touch your hand. →

2. if the tēacher says "stand up," touch your nōse. →

the fat ēagle →

an ēagle lĪked to ēat. hē āte cāke and ham and →

cōrn. hē āte and āte, and hē got fatter and fatter. →

hē said, "I am sō fat that I can not flȳ." →

hē sat in a trēē and the other ēagles māde fun of →

him. they said, "look at that fat, fat ēagle. hō, hō."

but then a tīger cāme hunting fōr ēagles. a little ēagle sat under a trēē. the tīger went after the little ēagle. the other ēagles yelled and yelled, but the little ēagle did not hēar them.

stop

rēₐd the Ītems ➝

1. when the tēₐcher says "touch your fēēt," stand

up.

2. if the tēₐcher says "gō," touch your ēₐrs.

the fat ēₐgle ➝

a fat, fat ēₐgle was sitti͡ng in a trēē when a tīger

cāme hunti͡ng fōr ēₐgles. the tīger went after a

little ēₐgle that was sitti͡ng under the trēē. the other

ēagles yelled, but the little ēagle did not hēar them.

the fat, fat ēagle looked down and said, "I must sāve the little ēagle." sō hē jumped from the trēē. hē cāme down līke a fat rock on the tīger. and the tīger ran far awāy.

now the other ēagles do not māke fun of the fat, fat ēagle. they give him cāke and ham and cōrn.

this is the end.

r̄ead the Ītems →

l. if the tēₐcher says "touch your nōseₑ," touch →

your f̄ēēt. →

2. when the tēₐcher says "giveₑ mē your book," giveₑ →

the tēₐcher your book. →

a man līked to gō fast

a man līked to gō fast. hē went fast in his car. hē walked fast and hē ran fast. hē ēven talked fast. his wīfe did not līke him to gō sō fast. but hē went fast.

hē sat down to ēat an egg and a fish cāke and a mēat pīe. but hē āte sō fast that the egg slipped and fell on his fēēt.

hē bent down fast and his nōse went into the ⟶

fish cāke. hē went to wīpe his nōse fast and hē hit ⟶

the mēat pīe. the mēat pīe hit his wīfe. ⟶

stop ⟶

read the items →

1. when the teacher says "touch your head," hold up
   your hands.

2. if the teacher picks up a book, say "now."

a man liked to go fast →

a man did things fast. he went fast in his

car. he walked fast. he talked fast. he even ate fast.

and when he ate, he got egg on his feet and fish cake

on his nōse.

the man said, "I will slōw down. I will not do things fast."

sō the man did not gō fast in his car. hē did not walk fast. hē did not talk fast. and hē did not ēat sō fast that hē got fish cāke on his nōse.

this is the end.